W9-BEV-306

I Can Draw...
Dinosaurs

Artwork by Terry Longhurst

Text by Amanda O'Neill

p

This is a Parragon Publishing Book
This edition published in 2002

Parragon Publishing
Queen Street House
4 Queen Street
Bath BA1 1HE, UK

Copyright © Parragon 2001

Designed, packaged, and produced by
Touchstone

ISBN 0-75257-277-6

Artwork by Terry Longhurst
Text by Amanda O'Neill
Edited by Philip de Ste. Croix

Printed in Dubai, U.A.E

About this book

Everybody can enjoy drawing, but sometimes it's hard to know where to begin. The subject you want to draw can look very complicated. This book shows you how to start, by breaking down your subject into a series of simple shapes.

The tools you need are very simple. The basic requirements are paper and pencils. Very thin paper wears through if you have to rub out a line, so choose paper that is thick enough to work on. Pencils come with different leads, from very hard to very soft. Very hard pencils give a clean, thin line which is best for finishing drawings. Very soft ones give a thicker, darker line. You will probably find a medium pencil most useful.

If you want to color in your drawing, you have the choice of paints, colored inks, or felt-tip pens. Fine felt-tips are useful for drawing outlines, thick felt-tips are better for coloring in.

The most important tool you have is your own eyes. The mistake many people make is to draw what they think something looks like, instead of really looking at it carefully first. Half the secret of making your drawing look good is getting the proportions right. Study your subject before you start, and break it down in your mind into sections. Check how much bigger, or longer, or shorter, one part is than another. Notice where one part joins another, and at what angle. See where there are flowing curves, and where there are straight lines.

The step-by-step drawings in this book show you exactly how to do this. Each subject is broken down into easy stages, so you can build up your drawing one piece at a time. Look carefully at each shape before – and after – you draw it. If you find you have drawn it the wrong size or in the wrong place, correct it before you go on. Then the next shape will fit into place, and piece-by-piece you can build up a fantastic picture.

Stegosaurus

This giant plant-eater was well protected against enemies. It was the size of a tank, armor-plated, and armed with a spiked tail. The big upright plates down its back may have been just for display, to make it look even bigger, or they may have been solar panels, to soak up the Sun's heat.

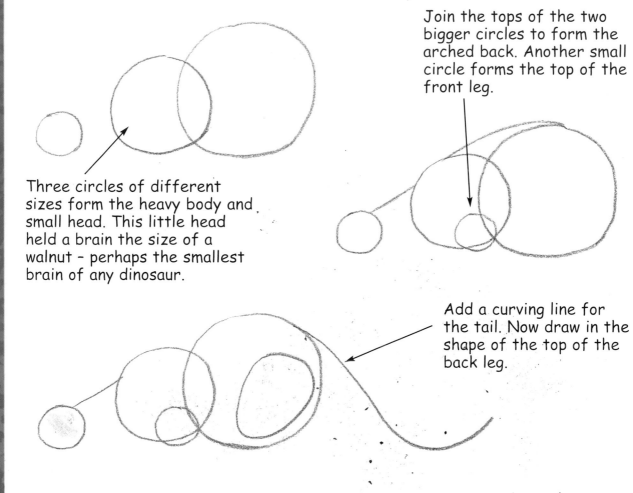

Join the tops of the two bigger circles to form the arched back. Another small circle forms the top of the front leg.

Three circles of different sizes form the heavy body and small head. This little head held a brain the size of a walnut – perhaps the smallest brain of any dinosaur.

Add a curving line for the tail. Now draw in the shape of the top of the back leg.

Finish off the body shape and add the first row of back plates, making them bigger as you go up the body. Shape the head and tail.

Long sharp spikes make the tail a deadly weapon for self-defense.

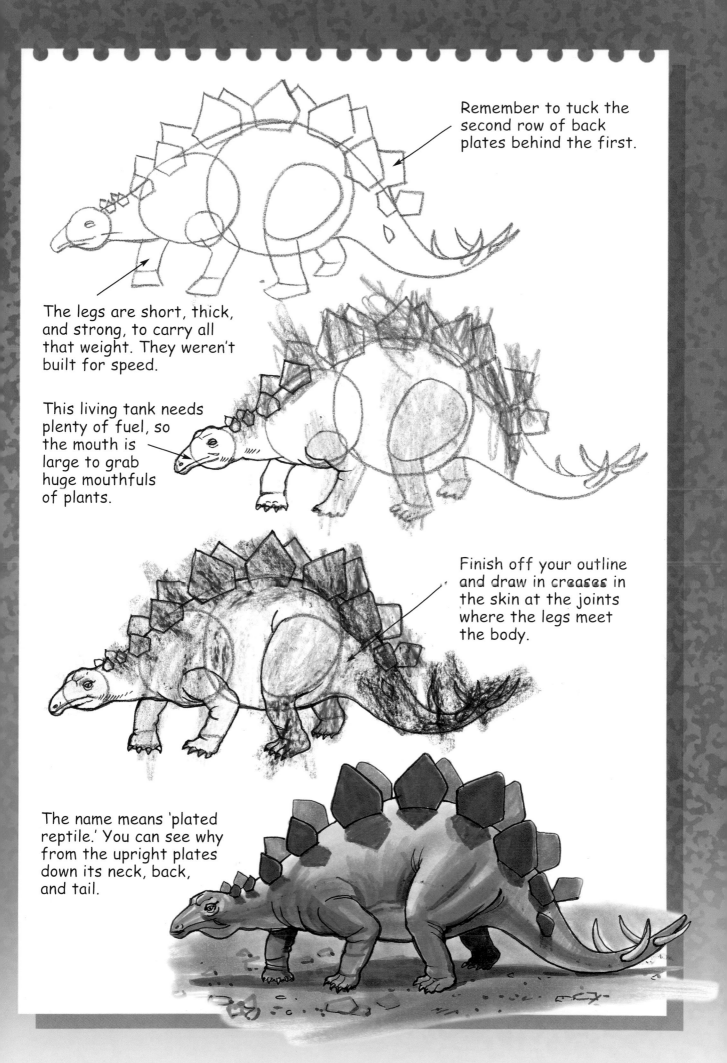

Remember to tuck the second row of back plates behind the first.

The legs are short, thick, and strong, to carry all that weight. They weren't built for speed.

This living tank needs plenty of fuel, so the mouth is large to grab huge mouthfuls of plants.

Finish off your outline and draw in creases in the skin at the joints where the legs meet the body.

The name means 'plated reptile.' You can see why from the upright plates down its neck, back, and tail.

Tyrannosaurus

Tyrannosaurus was one of the biggest meat-eaters ever to live on Earth. It was so tall that a man would only come up to its knee, and it weighed as much as seven automobiles. It ran on two powerful legs to chase its prey, and its mouth was armed with teeth each as long as a man's hand.

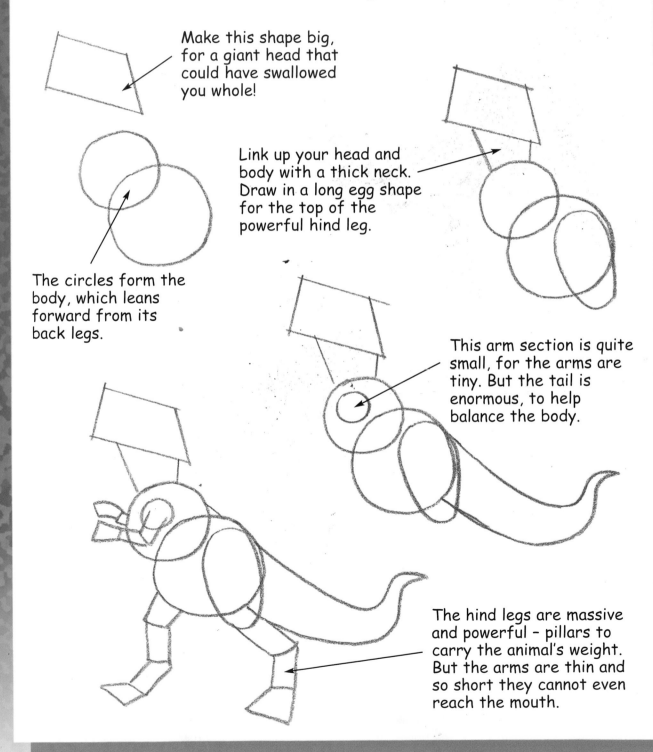

Make this shape big, for a giant head that could have swallowed you whole!

Link up your head and body with a thick neck. Draw in a long egg shape for the top of the powerful hind leg.

The circles form the body, which leans forward from its back legs.

This arm section is quite small, for the arms are tiny. But the tail is enormous, to help balance the body.

The hind legs are massive and powerful – pillars to carry the animal's weight. But the arms are thin and so short they cannot even reach the mouth.

Finish off the head with an eye and two rows of sharp teeth.

The useless-looking arms end in hands with long clawed fingers.

Finish off your outline. The hind feet stand on three strong toes with large claws.

The name means 'tyrant reptile.' A tyrant is a cruel ruler, and the other dinosaurs on which Tyrannosaurus preyed must have found that it really lived up to its name.

Deinonychus

Deinonychus means 'terrible claw' and the long claw on its hind foot was a truly terrible weapon. The clawed toe operated on a special hinge to slash down like a knife. This meat-eater was quite small for a dinosaur – not much taller than a man. It probably hunted in packs to tackle large prey.

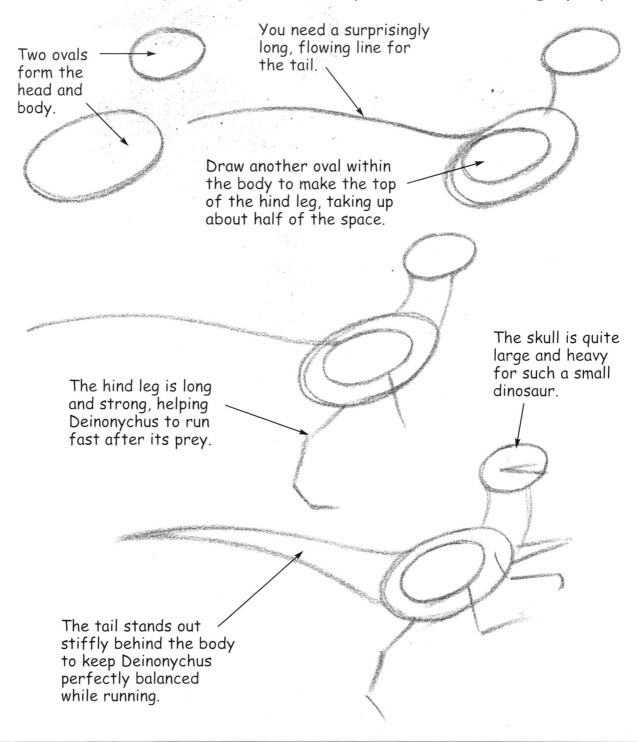

Two ovals form the head and body.

You need a surprisingly long, flowing line for the tail.

Draw another oval within the body to make the top of the hind leg, taking up about half of the space.

The hind leg is long and strong, helping Deinonychus to run fast after its prey.

The skull is quite large and heavy for such a small dinosaur.

The tail stands out stiffly behind the body to keep Deinonychus perfectly balanced while running.

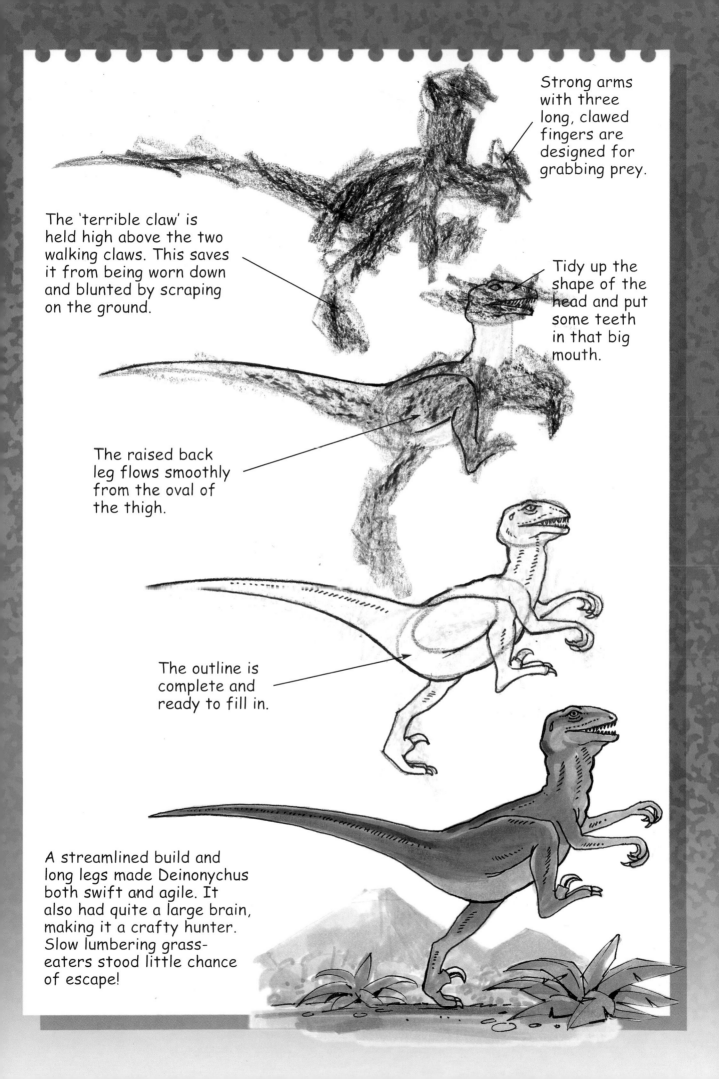

Strong arms with three long, clawed fingers are designed for grabbing prey.

The 'terrible claw' is held high above the two walking claws. This saves it from being worn down and blunted by scraping on the ground.

Tidy up the shape of the head and put some teeth in that big mouth.

The raised back leg flows smoothly from the oval of the thigh.

The outline is complete and ready to fill in.

A streamlined build and long legs made Deinonychus both swift and agile. It also had quite a large brain, making it a crafty hunter. Slow lumbering grass-eaters stood little chance of escape!

Triceratops

Despite its fearsome appearance, Triceratops was a harmless plant-eater. The huge horns that give it its name ('three-horned face') were for defense, not attack. The huge bony frill behind its head was also protection, guarding its neck from attack from behind.

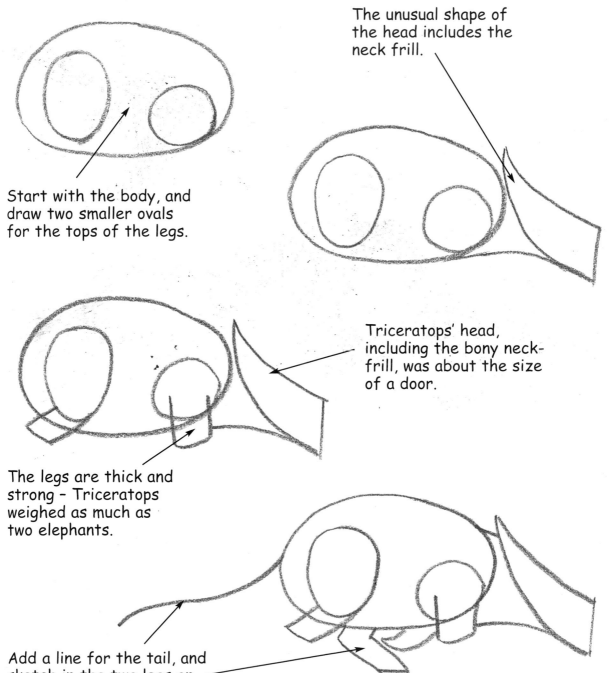

Start with the body, and draw two smaller ovals for the tops of the legs.

The unusual shape of the head includes the neck frill.

Triceratops' head, including the bony neck-frill, was about the size of a door.

The legs are thick and strong – Triceratops weighed as much as two elephants.

Add a line for the tail, and sketch in the two legs on the other side of the body.

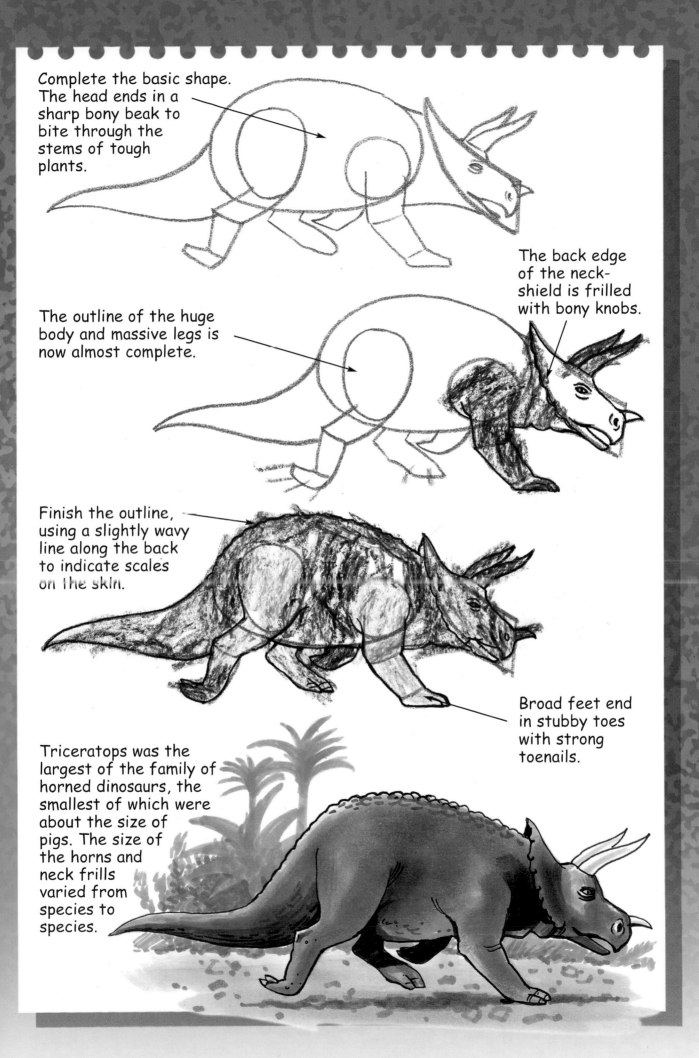

Complete the basic shape. The head ends in a sharp bony beak to bite through the stems of tough plants.

The back edge of the neck-shield is frilled with bony knobs.

The outline of the huge body and massive legs is now almost complete.

Finish the outline, using a slightly wavy line along the back to indicate scales on the skin.

Broad feet end in stubby toes with strong toenails.

Triceratops was the largest of the family of horned dinosaurs, the smallest of which were about the size of pigs. The size of the horns and neck frills varied from species to species.

Hadrosaur

Hadrosaurs are nicknamed 'duckbilled dinosaurs' because of their broad horny beaks. They are also known as 'helmet heads' from their strange crests. There were several species with differing crests: this one also has a backward-pointing horn on its head.

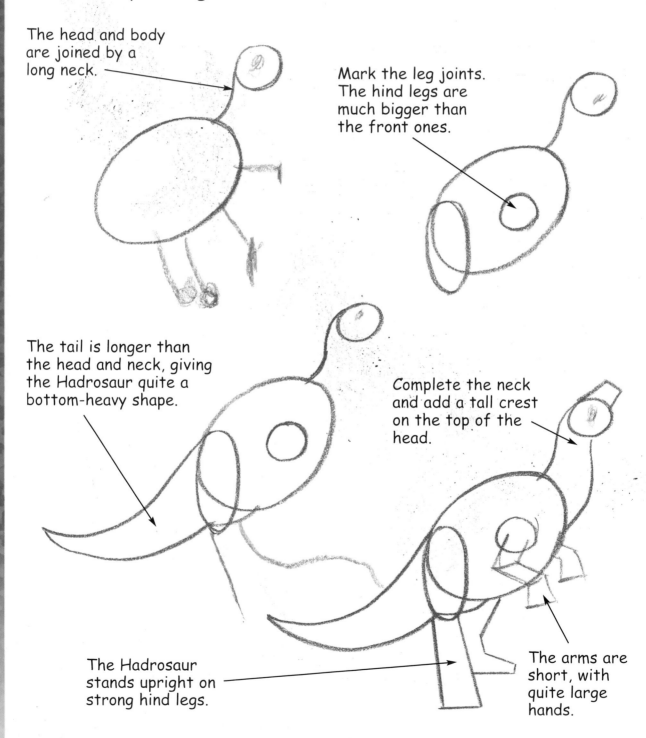

The head and body are joined by a long neck.

Mark the leg joints. The hind legs are much bigger than the front ones.

The tail is longer than the head and neck, giving the Hadrosaur quite a bottom-heavy shape.

Complete the neck and add a tall crest on the top of the head.

The Hadrosaur stands upright on strong hind legs.

The arms are short, with quite large hands.

Complete the head shape by adding the horn and beak.

Draw in the shape of the hind leg and the broad toes.

Finish the outlines of head and neck. A little shading makes the neck look much more solid.

The crest was probably a sort of trumpet! It was hollow, and the dinosaur's breathing tubes ran through it. When it blew down its nose, it would have produced a loud booming noise.

Fill in the rest of the outline and add more shading.

The various species of Hadrosaur were all plant eaters. This one tackled its food with jaws like grindstones, fitted out with hundreds of tiny teeth to mash up tough stems.

Parksosaurus

Not all dinosaurs were giants, and this one, if you ignore the tail, was only about the size of a big dog. In many ways it was the dinosaur version of today's deer and antelopes: a plant-eater, it lived in herds, and relied on its speed to escape enemies.

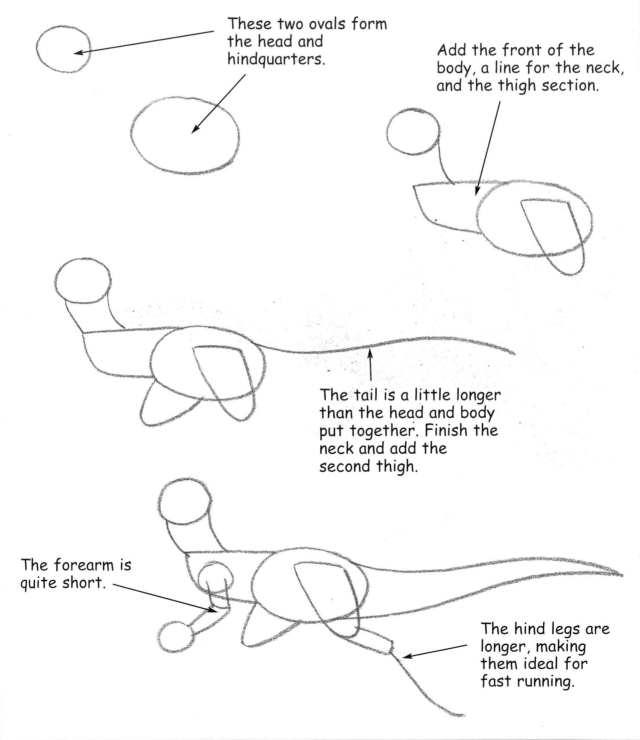

These two ovals form the head and hindquarters.

Add the front of the body, a line for the neck, and the thigh section.

The tail is a little longer than the head and body put together. Finish the neck and add the second thigh.

The forearm is quite short.

The hind legs are longer, making them ideal for fast running.

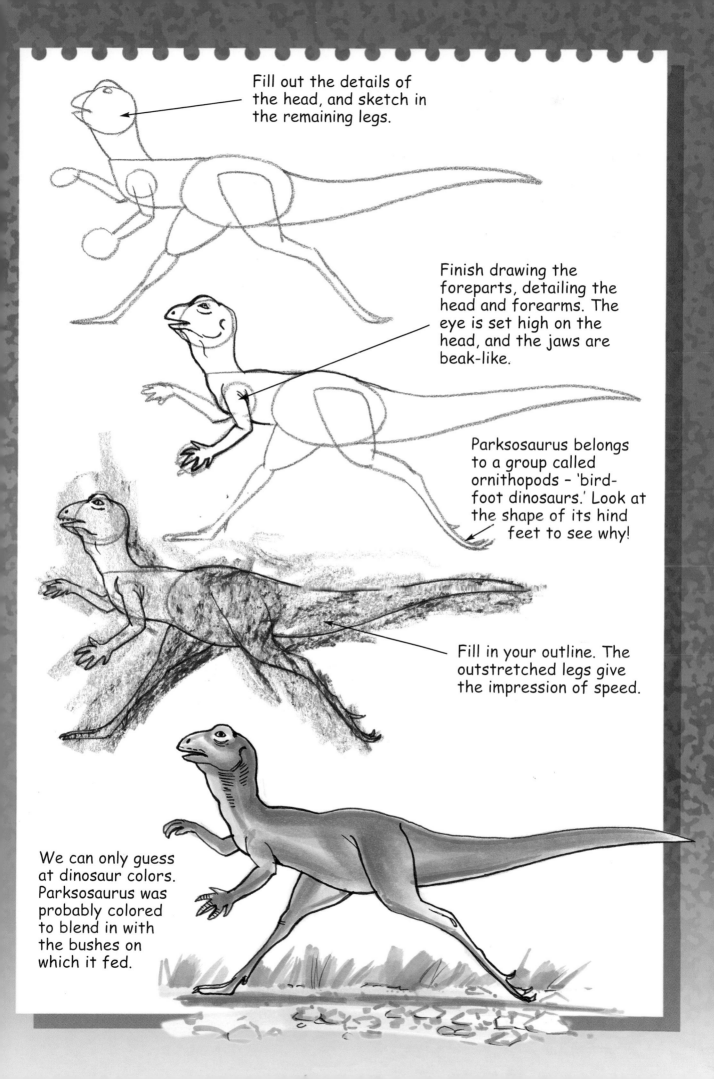

Fill out the details of the head, and sketch in the remaining legs.

Finish drawing the foreparts, detailing the head and forearms. The eye is set high on the head, and the jaws are beak-like.

Parksosaurus belongs to a group called ornithopods – 'bird-foot dinosaurs.' Look at the shape of its hind feet to see why!

Fill in your outline. The outstretched legs give the impression of speed.

We can only guess at dinosaur colors. Parksosaurus was probably colored to blend in with the bushes on which it fed.

Parasaurolophus

Parasaurolophus had perhaps the oddest head of any dinosaur. Its long narrow crest stuck out for about six feet beyond the back of its head. With air passages running through it, the crest probably helped the dinosaur to make sounds.

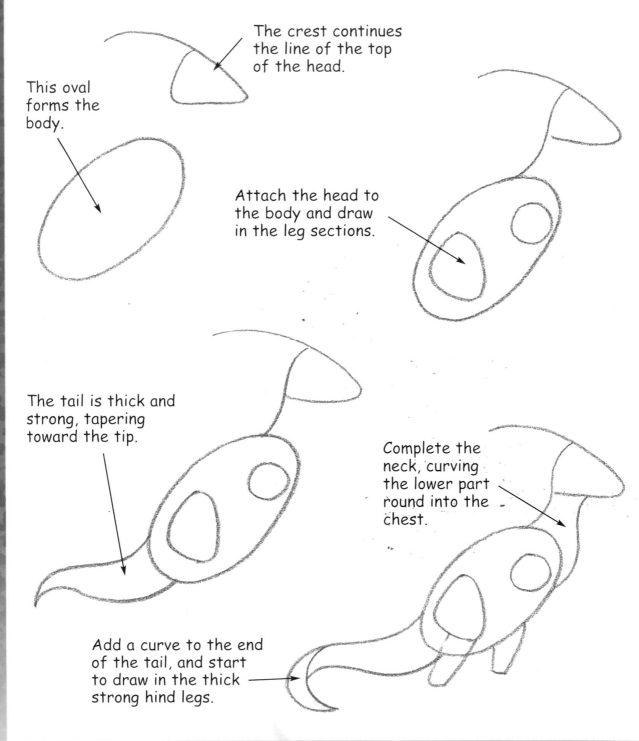

The crest continues the line of the top of the head.

This oval forms the body.

Attach the head to the body and draw in the leg sections.

The tail is thick and strong, tapering toward the tip.

Complete the neck, curving the lower part round into the chest.

Add a curve to the end of the tail, and start to draw in the thick strong hind legs.

Draw in the legs to complete the shape, and start sketching in the face.

The crest runs all the way down to the nostrils.

Sturdy legs and feet support the weight.

Draw in the toes, which are quite long.

Now you can ink over your final lines, remembering to keep the curves smooth.

Scientists once thought the crest was a snorkel to help the dinosaur swim underwater – until they realized it had no hole in it to let air in!

Pteranodon

When dinosaurs ruled the Earth, flying reptiles, or pterosaurs, ruled the skies. They came in many shapes and sizes. Some were as small as sparrows, but Pteranodon was a giant, about the size of a glider. In fact, scientists think it flew by gliding – it was probably too big to flap its wings.

These two shapes will form the body and hind legs.

The head, with its open jaws, will fit into this long box shape.

A long bony crest probably helped to balance the heavy head in flight.

The legs are tiny – not the legs of a creature that does much walking.

Add the first wing. It is made of leathery skin attached to the arm and finger bones.

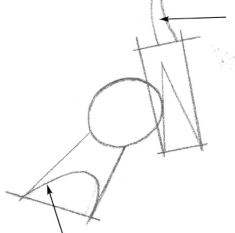

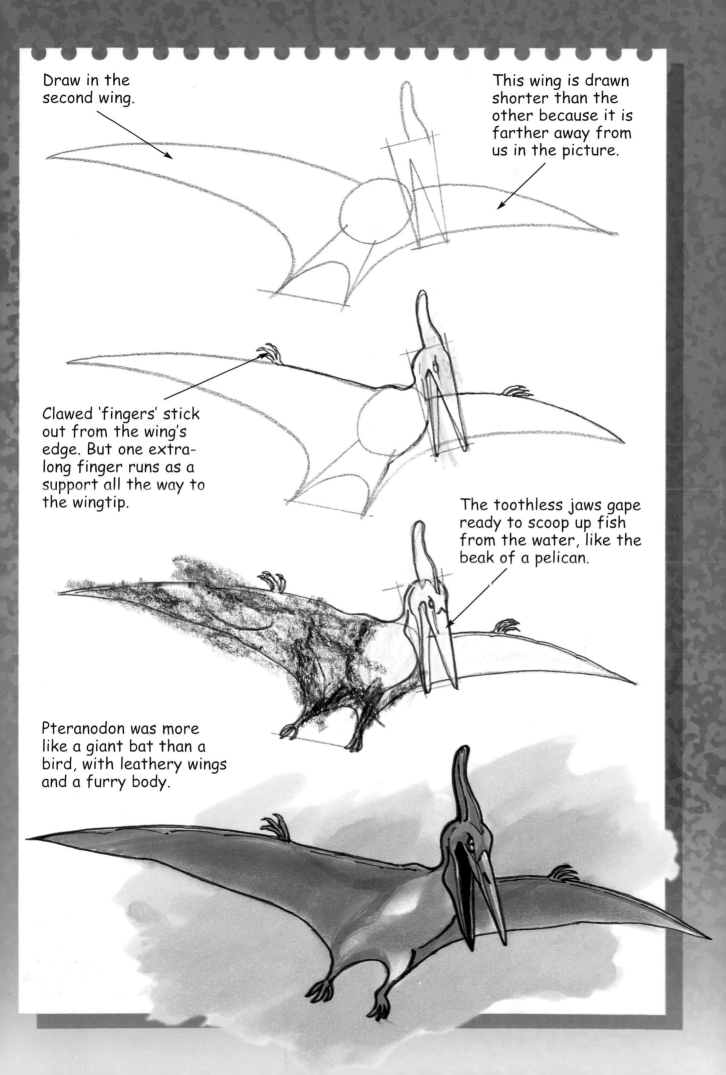

Draw in the second wing.

This wing is drawn shorter than the other because it is farther away from us in the picture.

Clawed 'fingers' stick out from the wing's edge. But one extra-long finger runs as a support all the way to the wingtip.

The toothless jaws gape ready to scoop up fish from the water, like the beak of a pelican.

Pteranodon was more like a giant bat than a bird, with leathery wings and a furry body.

Camptosaurus

This big, slow-moving plant-eater probably spent most of its time on all fours. But when danger threatened, it ran on two legs. It could also rear up on its hind legs to reach high branches, and then its smaller forelegs served as arms to grasp the food.

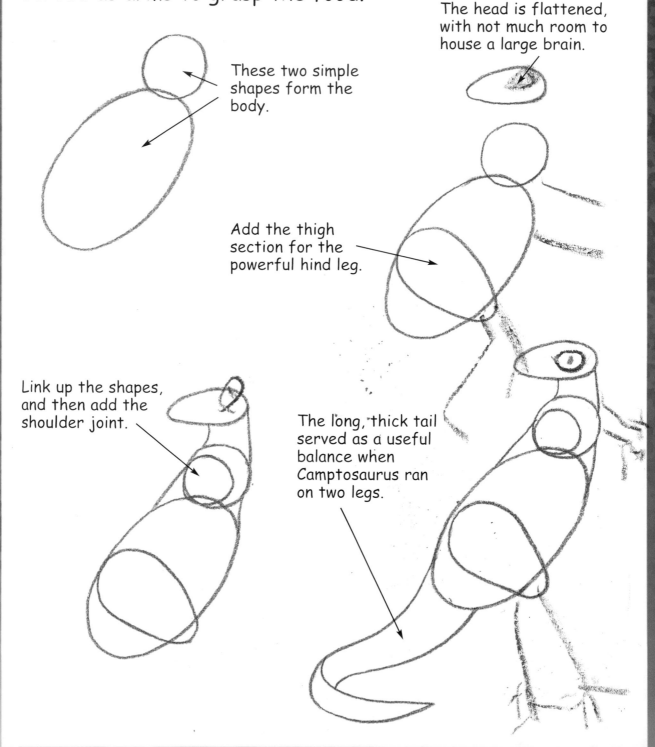

These two simple shapes form the body.

The head is flattened, with not much room to house a large brain.

Add the thigh section for the powerful hind leg.

Link up the shapes, and then add the shoulder joint.

The long, thick tail served as a useful balance when Camptosaurus ran on two legs.

Finish off the initial sketch by completing the legs and marking out eyes and mouth.

Now the head needs attention. Make the jaws a little narrower than in your first shape.

Now you can ink in the whole outline.

The jaws have hard, beak-like edges for cutting through tough plant stems.

Compsognathus

Not all dinosaurs were giants: this little hunter was about the size of a small dog, and lived on small prey like insects and lizards. It swallowed its food whole – in fact, the first Compsognathus fossil ever found had a whole lizard skeleton lying in its stomach.

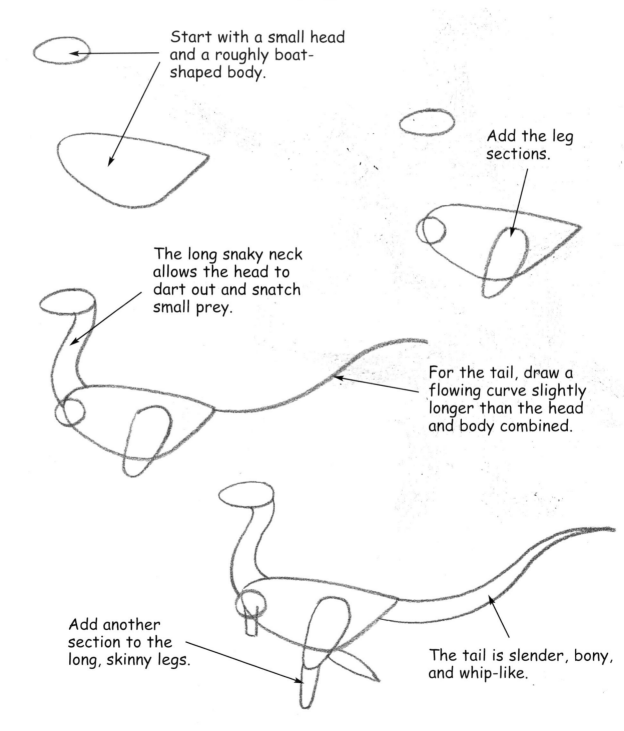

Start with a small head and a roughly boat-shaped body.

Add the leg sections.

The long snaky neck allows the head to dart out and snatch small prey.

For the tail, draw a flowing curve slightly longer than the head and body combined.

Add another section to the long, skinny legs.

The tail is slender, bony, and whip-like.

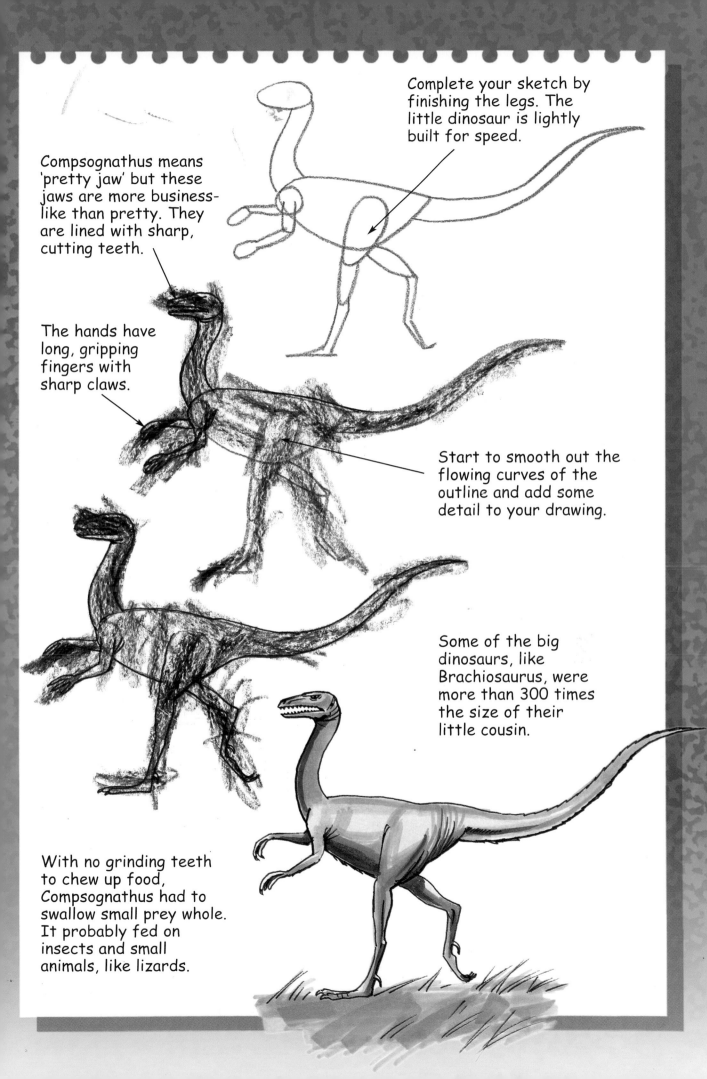

Complete your sketch by finishing the legs. The little dinosaur is lightly built for speed.

Compsognathus means 'pretty jaw' but these jaws are more business-like than pretty. They are lined with sharp, cutting teeth.

The hands have long, gripping fingers with sharp claws.

Start to smooth out the flowing curves of the outline and add some detail to your drawing.

Some of the big dinosaurs, like Brachiosaurus, were more than 300 times the size of their little cousin.

With no grinding teeth to chew up food, Compsognathus had to swallow small prey whole. It probably fed on insects and small animals, like lizards.

Hydrotherosaurus

Here we have a real 'sea monster.' It belonged to the family of plesiosaurs ('ribbon reptiles' – from their long, narrow shape), which were all adapted to a life at sea. It swam like a fish, but, unlike a fish, had to come to the surface to breathe.

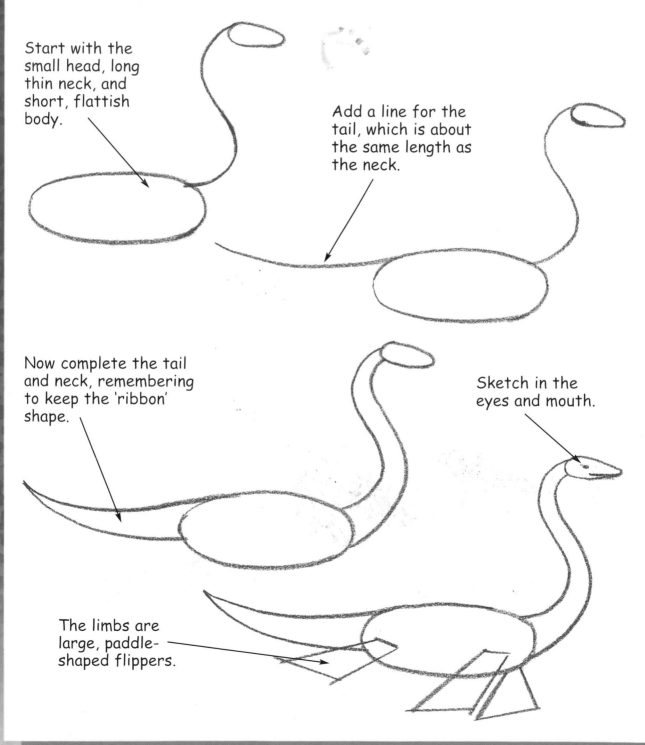

Start with the small head, long thin neck, and short, flattish body.

Add a line for the tail, which is about the same length as the neck.

Now complete the tail and neck, remembering to keep the 'ribbon' shape.

Sketch in the eyes and mouth.

The limbs are large, paddle-shaped flippers.

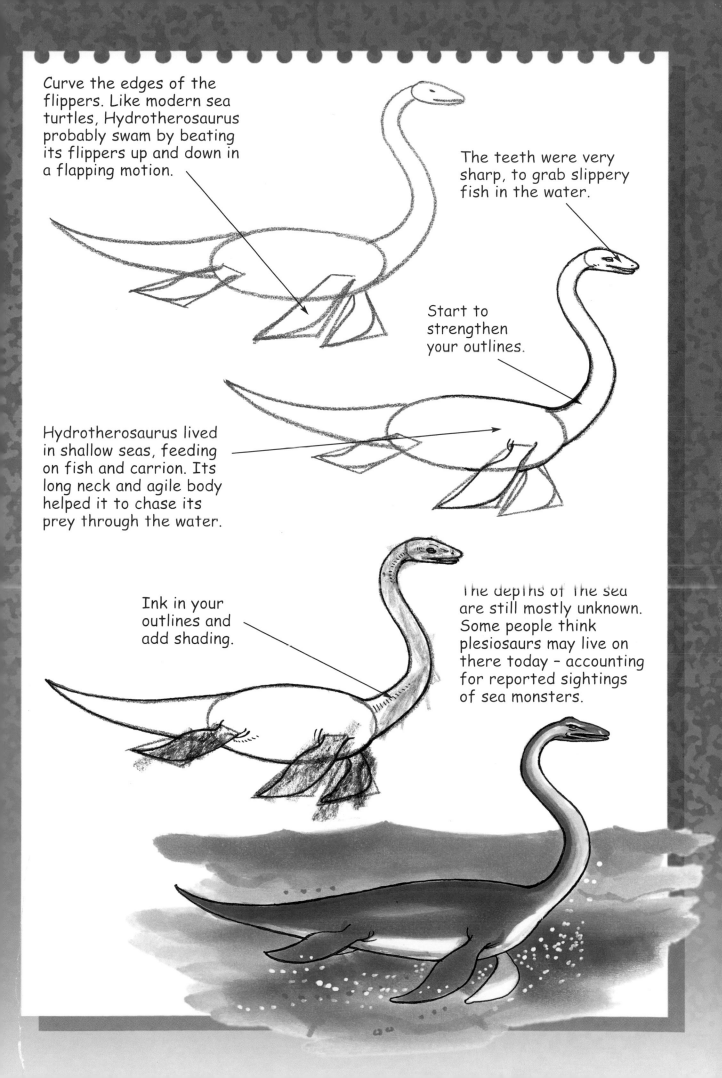

Curve the edges of the flippers. Like modern sea turtles, Hydrotherosaurus probably swam by beating its flippers up and down in a flapping motion.

The teeth were very sharp, to grab slippery fish in the water.

Start to strengthen your outlines.

Hydrotherosaurus lived in shallow seas, feeding on fish and carrion. Its long neck and agile body helped it to chase its prey through the water.

Ink in your outlines and add shading.

The depths of the sea are still mostly unknown. Some people think plesiosaurs may live on there today – accounting for reported sightings of sea monsters.

Diplodocus

Diplodocus was not the biggest dinosaur, but it was one of the longest. It was as long as a tennis court, though most of its length was neck and tail. It was built like a suspension bridge, with its long body supported on column-like legs.

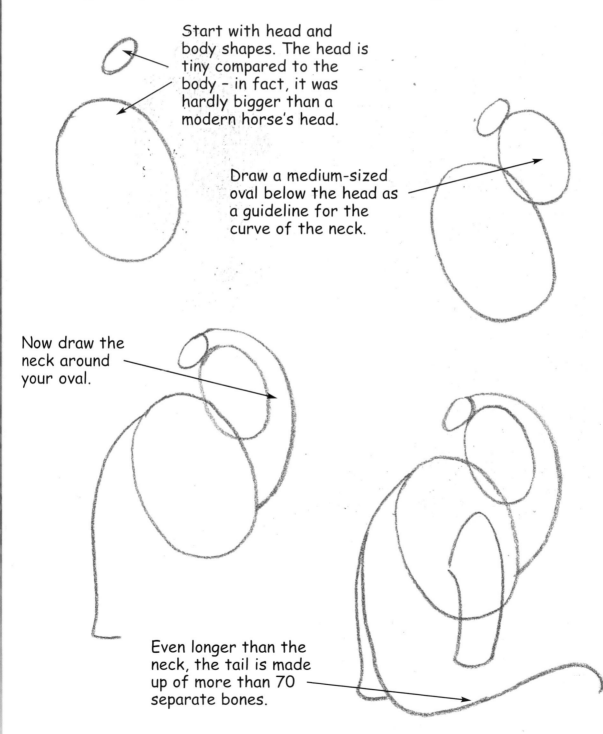

Start with head and body shapes. The head is tiny compared to the body – in fact, it was hardly bigger than a modern horse's head.

Draw a medium-sized oval below the head as a guideline for the curve of the neck.

Now draw the neck around your oval.

Even longer than the neck, the tail is made up of more than 70 separate bones.

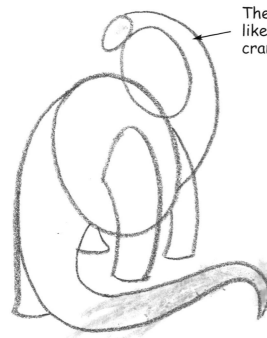

The long neck had muscles like the steel cables of a crane to help lift the head.

The jaws had teeth only at the front, to strip leaves from branches. Diplodocus must have spent its whole life eating, to take in enough food for its needs!

Ink in your outlines, adding shading to give weight to the huge legs and tail.

This huge plant-eater lived around 150 million years ago. Its name means 'double beam' – it refers to the shape of its tail bones.

Ornithomimus

This elegant little hunter was the dinosaur version of a modern ostrich – in fact its name means 'bird-mimic.' Like an ostrich, it was a fast runner, depending on its speed to escape enemies. It probably lived on insects, lizards – and other dinosaurs' eggs.

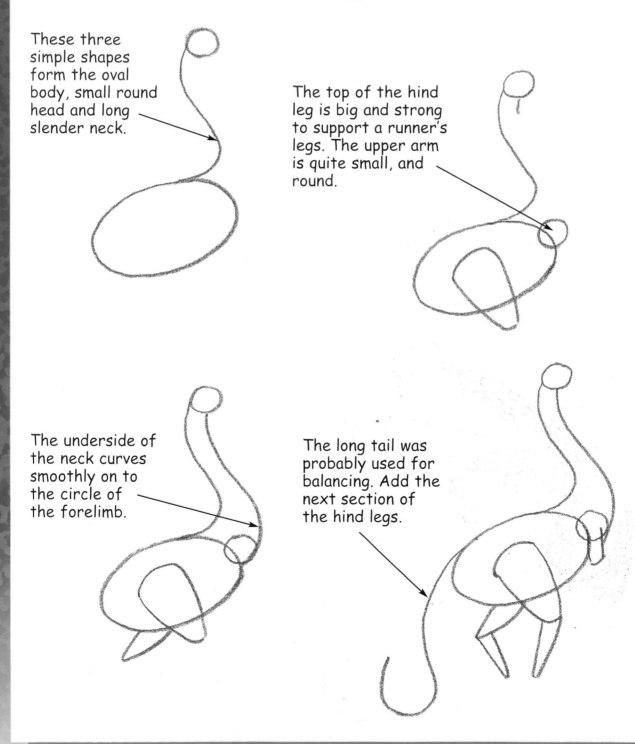

These three simple shapes form the oval body, small round head and long slender neck.

The top of the hind leg is big and strong to support a runner's legs. The upper arm is quite small, and round.

The underside of the neck curves smoothly on to the circle of the forelimb.

The long tail was probably used for balancing. Add the next section of the hind legs.

Finish the stilt-like legs, long arms, and strong tail. Give the tiny head a bird-like beak.

The head really does look like a bird's. The eyes are large, like an ostrich's. Ornithomimus had no teeth, pecking at food with its sharp-edged beak instead.

Start to ink in your outline.

Add a little shading to give the body form and solidity.

Ornithomimus had no natural weapons to defend itself against the giant meat-eaters that hunted it. But its speed and agility would usually have kept it out of trouble.

Maiasaura

Maiasaura got its name, 'good mother reptile,' from the discovery of its 'nursery.' This species lived in groups. The females built earth-mound nests in which they laid their eggs, and guarded their young until the baby dinosaurs could look after themselves.

Two simple shapes form the head and body.

Draw the neck, and add the thigh of the hind leg.

The head is long, and rather horse-like.

A thick, strong tail helps to balance the body.

This shape will give you the right angle for both the front legs.

Draw in the rear legs. They are slightly bent and end with large toes.

Now the rough outline is complete, you can see that Maiasaura would have been too heavy to sit on her eggs. But the earth kept the eggs warm – until they hatched.

Finish off the head, and draw the face with a wide, plant-eater's mouth.

Now you can finish your drawing. Add shading, and give a bit of a ridge to the spine.

Maiasaura belonged to the hadrosaur family – the 'duckbilled dinosaurs.' It was about as long as two family cars, and fed on plants.